easily resolved as soon as we establish an understanding— and applying this understanding in a practical way. A terrarium must meet the needs of the forms of life we are interested in. Boiled down to an example, no one can establish an environment for a desert tortoise that will also support a newt or a salamander. A desert tortoise will develop fungal diseases and surely die if it isn't permitted to remain quite dry at least nine days out of every ten. A newt or a salamander would surely shrivel up, dry out, and die under those same conditions. Yes, you can easily maintain desert tortoises and moss-dwelling newts in home terrariums, but you cannot maintain a desert tortoise and a newt in the same terrarium at the same time. No way!

Think of it this way: you want to admire, enjoy, study, show off, tame, and possibly even breed an animal or a group of *similar* animals in a terrarium. Can you succeed? Yes, certainly! How about adding some additional plants or animals that inhabit other environmental niches? Can you still succeed? No, absolutely not! Your entire establishment will rot, shrivel, stink, starve, or otherwise fail. Your pets will

surely die and your enthusiasm will soon fade.

Apart from considerations of expense, it is a sad thing to capture an animal, whether it is a frog or a lizard or whatever, and then hold it captive under the wrong conditions until it dies of disease or starvation. Where do you want to draw the line? Insects? Fishes? Cage birds? Farm animals? Cats and dogs? People?

Put aside the financial and humane considerations and let's just concentrate on establishing and maintaining a tiny three-dimensional living segment of the natural world. Here we can watch at home what we might never otherwise see. People have been doing this sort of thing for centuries and most of the procedures are simple to explain and easy to perform. Try it; you'll like it.

One example of a terrarium for tarantulas. Before acquiring any terrarium animal, learn about its environmental needs.

3

GETTING STARTED

Green anole, *Anolis carolinensis*. This species is often called the American chameleon; in most cases individuals will not survive more than three years in captivity.

When all else fails, start over, but this time begin by reading the instructions. For terrarium keepers, the instruction list is relatively short and deceptively simple. Many of us conclude that we are experts long before we served any time as apprentices. This is not the time or place to change human nature, but perhaps the mention of a few of these deceptively

simple items could help you to really enjoy your hobby.

• Obtain the largest aquarium or cage you can handle and afford. Many problems are caused by crowding plants or animals.

• For starters, begin with a dry woodland or, better still, a desert habitat. Waste products such as uneaten food or feces will decay and smell if they are

TERRARIUMS
FOR YOUR NEW PET

MERVIN F. ROBERTS

8
of Herptiles, 19

, 63

xelrod, William B. Allen Jr., Tom
;eorge Dibley, Dr. Guido Dingerkus,
Isabelle Francais, Michael Gilroy,
ıhl, R.J. Koestler, J.K. Langhammer,
rium), S. McKeown, John M.
ıron Norman, L. Peter Pritchard,
ings by Scott Boldt, Richard
ın.

cations, Inc.

'ES by T.F.H. Publications, Inc., One T.F.H.
CANADA to the Pet Trade by H & L Pet
nt, Kitchener, Ontario N2B 2T6; Rolf C.
Montreal 382 Quebec; in CANADA to the
ıda (A Division of Canada Publishing
ıulevard, Agincourt, Ontario M1S 3C7; in
s, The Spinney, Parklands, Portsmouth PO7
SOUTH PACIFIC by T.F.H. (Australia) Pty.
S.W., Australia; in NEW ZEALAND by Ross
h Knox Place, Panmure, Auckland, New
Bio-Research, 5 Lippay Street, San Lorenzo
AFRICA by Multipet Pty. Ltd., P.O. Box
rica. Published by T.F.H. Publications, Inc.
of America by T.F.H. Publications, Inc.

① INTRODUCTION

Head study of a green or common iguana, *Iguana iguana*. This species is one of the most commonly seen lizards in captivity.

What is a terrarium? Ask five people, get five or six answers. On the other hand, most of us have no trouble defining an aquarium. We could say that it is a container of water arranged to support aquatic life. It is water-tight and it has at least one glass window. So then, what is so difficult about defining a terrarium? *Terra* refers to earth in the same way that *aqua* refers to water. The awkwardness that some of us need to understand concerns the degree of wetness and of water-tightness in a terrarium.

The reason for bringing up this stuffy bit of language early on is that many terrariums turn out to be smelly death traps for the very plants and animals we want to maintain and display. The problem and its solution are

Be sure your terrarium includes a water dish, hiding places, and something on which the animal can climb.

moist, but if they dry out quickly there will be less smell and less disease, especially fungal disease.

• Provide an arrangement that permits an animal to find a spot it likes. Offer it bright warmth and cooler darkness. Offer it perches and also things to crawl under. This helps to explain why a relatively large terrarium is desirable.

• Furnish a water container so large that the largest animal can crawl into it. This container must be so heavy that no creature can overturn it. This container must be easy for you to remove, sterilize, refill, and replace in the terrarium. This container must be absolutely leakproof. This container must have an inside surface that permits your pet to crawl out. This container could easily give you more trouble than any other part of the entire arrangement.

• Choose animals and plants to fit the environment you are providing. There is no moss in a desert and no cactus in a semiaquatic or bog habitat. How about artificial plants? Great. No problem. How about artificial animals? Great, they go well with artificial plants.

• Start slowly and keep the animal population small in size and in numbers and in cost. Under ideal conditions an iguana will live 20 years and grow to a length of 6 feet. A caiman will live even longer and grow even larger. Plan ahead. You will be amazed to discover how difficult it is to give away a 6-foot caiman.

• Pay special attention to the cover on your terrarium. These animals don't have much to occupy their minds except eating and escaping.

• Pay special attention to the cover on your terrarium, particularly if you have other pets in the house. Watch out especially for cats and four-year old children.

• Buy your livestock from an experienced, established pet dealer. Be prepared to pay a fair price for a healthy, lively animal *that you have watched while it was eating.* Sick or sickly or otherwise undesirable animals don't eat or don't eat avidly. Even a clumsy turtle, if it is healthy, eats avidly.

• Choose a small number, preferably just one to start, of animals that will not dominate or eat each other.

• Choose species that you can conveniently feed. For example, anoles require live insects. If you cannot keep live fruitflies and/or live mealworms in your home, then you cannot keep an anole alive. In that case, start with a turtle or an iguana that eats vegetables.

• After you have read this book and chosen an animal you are interested in, read some detailed literature about that animal. There is at least one book or booklet or technical paper on just about every living creature on God's green earth.

• Avoid dangerous animals. You are always at risk morally and legally if your pet hurts someone—even if that someone forced the lid off the cage and tried to pick up a venomous snake or a toxic toad or a nippy lizard. Even if that stupid person was properly warned!

• Be prepared to pay for professional help if your pet becomes sick. A veterinarian must be paid for his services— don't get the idea that you must pay for horses, dogs, and cats but turtles are free. If your veterinarian cannot treat an animal, he will tell you so.

• Don't let this list frighten you. There are tens of thousands of terrariums with thriving, attractive, odorless colonies of plants and animals providing enjoyment and new vistas to people all over the world.

Before purchasing your prospective pet, watch it eat. A creature with a healthy appetite is apt to have good health in general.

TERRARIUM HABITATS

If you are reading this book, you probably started with an animal and now you want to do the right thing by it. The project would have been a bit easier on you and on the animal if you had started with the book and then established a suitable habitat before you got the pet, but no matter, where there is life, there is hope.

What have you got? What are its natural habitat, food, temperature range, preferred humidity, light, and other requirements? Yes, you can carry an anole on your shoulder fastened to your shirt by a tiny chain, but that isn't what this book is all about. We should start with the categories of habitat and some of the animals and plants that do well as terrarium inhabitants in each of the habitats. First consider the big picture. Later we will get into the fine points and details.

Basic Habitats

Desert: hot days, cold nights, infrequent precipitation.

Temperate woodland: moist

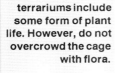

The most attractive terrariums include some form of plant life. However, do not overcrowd the cage with flora.

but not wet surface, bark and twigs and green plants.

Temperate semiaquatic: both dry perches and swimming areas.

Tropical woodland: bark and twigs and green plants, but warmer and in some instances more humid than temperate woodland.

Tropical semiaquatic: warmer than temperate semiaquatic.

A terrarium consists of plants and animals in a container that separates them from the container's surroundings and permits you to manipulate the internal environment (moisture, temperature, and light). What animal life you introduce is your business. You have every right to create a terrarium for land hermit crabs or land crabs or scorpions or tarantulas or hamsters or gerbils or reptiles or amphibians. Most terrariums are set up for reptiles or amphibians, but you should keep an open mind. Just remember that a tarantula will eat an anole and a hognosed snake will eat a toad, so you should think a little *before* you bring home your approximation of that famous painting "The Peaceable Kingdom." In point of fact, in the real world there is no such thing.

Desert

Desert plants do include yucca and sagebrush, but as a practical

matter most successful desert habitat terrariums are planted with cacti, snakeplants, aloe, and jade plants. They are furnished with sandy bottoms and rocky hiding places. You might well ask if an American chameleon is safe with those cactus spines. Well, no. To begin at the beginning, the American "chameleon" is an anole and not a chameleon. Also, it should be treated more like a tropical woodland animal and less like a desert animal. Many anoles die of thirst because their owners did not understand this fact of life. The cactus and the anole do not go together. The cactus, surely a desert plant, is better associated with the spiny lizards that many of us improperly call horned toads but which are officially horned lizards. Oh yes, there are also spiny lizards, another genus altogether. Confusing? Yes!

This, it seems, is as good a place as any to list just a few of

Keep in mind that most terrarium animals are predators in one way or another; therefore, a community cage is very difficult to achieve. Beginners should start out with one animal.

the creatures you might maintain in a desert terrarium environment. No matter how much money or space you have, you cannot assemble one of each in a single enclosure. Many eat or are eaten by many of the others. You will get to understand that aspect soon—surely, one would hope, before you put any more money down on the counter.

Tarantulas —Most species sold are really tropical woodland—associated with bananas—but they are sometimes kept in a desert setting. There are some truly desert-dwelling species also. This is an arthropod, not a vertebrate animal.

Scorpions —Most scorpions are truly desert animals. A scorpion, like the tarantula, is not a vertebrate animal but rather is an arthropod more nearly related to a horseshoe crab than to a lizard or even a spider.

Horned Lizards —Commonly called horned toads but truly lizards.

Spiny Lizards —There are about 15 species found in the southwestern U.S.A. and numerous subspecies that may be difficult to recognize.

Tortoises —When we say turtle or terrapin we imply dampness or ocean. When we say tortoise we suggest a dry environment.

Shovelnose snakes —Most species are strictly desert inhabitants.

Kangaroo rats —Most people think of a terrarium in terms of reptiles and amphibians, but really it is up to us to decide, isn't it? Just don't mix mammals with any other class of animals. They simply don't mix.

Gerbil —Surely another desert mammal. There is no reason why you cannot keep one in a cage or terrarium that resembles its natural habitat rather than in a plastic, tin, or cardboard arrangement.

Hamster —Like the gerbil and the kangaroo rats, the hamster is a desert mammal. Mammals like these use more energy and need more food than reptiles, so they might nibble some decorative plants if they are crowded or improperly fed.

A short digression is in order here—if you want a care-free, trouble-free view of nature, try a book or a photo or a framed picture or a video tape. If you want to watch a natural environment with living plants and animals that eat and grow and reproduce and defecate, then *you must thoughtfully exert yourself* to keep the system going. You must add food and clean water. You must remove excess food and wastes or install insects or land crabs or some other scavenger to do it for you. You will need to monitor temperature and humidity. The intensity and duration of light must also be under your control.

I don't recommend that anyone go out and buy a terrarium full of plants and animal life as an unsolicited gift for someone else. A terrarium is alive, like a pet, and it requires a commitment from a real live person to make it work.

The desert habitat will not sustain life without some moisture in some form at least sometime. The animals and plants that are adapted to desert life are great economizers. They require very little water. They may even convert some stored fat into water as they metabolize it during extended periods of drought. When you and I breathe, we exhale the nitrogen that is the major constituent of air, some unused oxygen, and carbon dioxide that we generated by our life processes. So also with water; not all of it passes out by way of the kidneys and bladder. Some ends up as perspiration and some may depart as moisture in our breath. Also, some people are prone to weep, especially when exposed to soap operas. By contrast, desert animals don't perspire or weep. Some even

Eastern newt, *Notophthalmus viridiscens viridiscens*. This is an immature newt, or eft.

retain more of the water vapor that we normally exhale as we breathe. Thus they manage to hang on to proportionately more of that moisture than you or I, and they thus can thrive where we might wither.

Can any animal absorb moisture through its skin? I have no evidence before me, but I have seen frogs and toads positively swell up as they sit in a puddle after the first rain following a dry spell. Also, I've never seen a frog or a toad stick out its tongue and lap up a drink. When it comes to reptiles, usually considered to be a notch or so higher on the evolutionary scale than amphibians, they seem to be mouth drinkers rather than skin suckers. The ever-popular

11

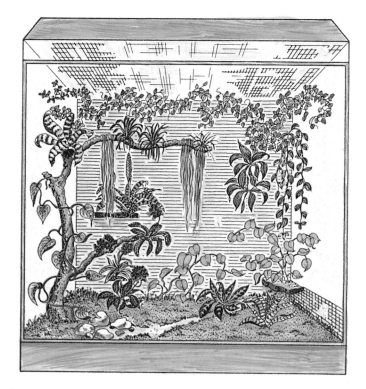

American anoles and their African counterparts, the true chameleons, surely lap up droplets of rain or dew. In fact, they cannot survive without moisture *in that form.* A dish of water in a terrarium with chameleons is meaningless except that it might trap some insects.

Of course, desert animals that eat succulent fruits, flowers, and other plants get most of their moisture that way. A cactus, once one gets past the spines, is positively juicy.

When the desert habitat is especially dry and hot for a prolonged period, some animals resort to a strategy that we call estivation. In science fiction there is frequently reference to suspended animation, which means just what it says: animate life does not proceed. There is no respiration or excretion or secretion or feeding or circulation or reproduction. This is entirely possible in science fiction, but most non-fiction scientists don't see suspended animation of higher animals as a way of life. For one thing, there is the matter of moisture retention, and for another there is the question of what happens to the bacteria in our digestive systems if *we* don't eat. What do the *bacteria* eat? If they don't eat, do they die or do they get suspended too? Well, Mother Nature does come close to suspended animation with desert animals. She gives them estivation. Life processes are not suspended but they are drastically slowed down. Heartbeat, respiration, and digestive processes all proceed, but at a very slow rate. Moisture loss is reduced, energy is conserved, and life awaits an improvement in the climate. You might think of estivation in a hot desert environment as a parallel to hibernation during a period of intense cold. Woodchucks and reptiles in northern climes hibernate; in the desert, tortoises and some toads estivate—occasionally in the same burrow.

Your desert terrarium need not provide facilities for animals to estivate, but you should be certain that the light or heat you provide is *not* uniform over the entire area occupied by the animals. By providing some variety in light and heat, you give your pet the opportunity to choose what it prefers. As time goes on you might want to make more of the habitat resemble the area where the animal spends most of its time.

Should you want to keep several animals in one terrarium there is always the risk of incompatibility. All of us have seen newspaper photos of cats nursing young rabbits and big mean dogs nursing kittens and circus elephants carrying tigers on their backs, but that's newspaper stuff and not real life In real life if you want healthy animals in your best approximation of their native habitat, you should confine yourself to one species per terrarium. A few same-size skinks will probably do well together. Add a snake and perhaps the smallest skink will be the first to go. That brings up another point. Every farmer or farmer's wife who ever kept chickens will tell you about the pecking order. One old rooster—the cock of the walk—will dominate the flock. The young cockerels will hang around but not closely. The senior hen will keep all the younger hens in line.

California newt, *Taricha torosa*. This species needs a large aqua-terrarium; it feeds on slugs and earthworms.

High school students have pecking orders and so do school teachers and so do lizards in a terrarium. If there is more than one, there surely will be one at the top of the pecking order *and* another at the bottom. If there is nowhere else to escape, it will

surely escape to Heaven.

Temperatures in the desert fluctuate widely. During the day the surface of the sand might be positively too hot to touch, and at night there could be a frost. How do the native cold-blooded animals survive these extremes? They burrow into the sand or hide in caves or under large rocks. How closely do you want to imitate nature? A perfectly "natural" desert terrarium would put the animals in hiding during the time you want to observe them, so there must be some

compromises. How well *you* compromise with Mother Nature will determine how well you succeed as a terrarium keeper.

The reason for starting the list of habitats with the desert is that it will prove to be the easiest for a beginner to maintain. I mentioned previously and here I repeat that decay, mildew, and many fungal diseases will not proceed in a dry environment.

As you become more experienced in this sort of pet keeping, surely you will branch out into woodland, semiaquatic, and even aquatic environments. There are many fascinating animals including softshelled turtles and clawed frogs that never or hardly ever leave the water.

Temperate Woodland

Here we find garter snakes, hognosed snakes, kingsnakes, milk snakes, green snakes—there are at least 30 species that you can purchase or perhaps catch, all of which will thrive in a temperate woodland terrarium environment. Here too you can keep the American toad and others of that genus, *Bufo*. Then there are the spadefoot toads, some of which will manage with even less moisture. The red eft—which is an immature red-spotted newt— will appear after rains in a temperate woodland setting, but when the American toad is comfortable this newt will probably be uncomfortably dry. Most newts and salamanders need a damper environment.

The turtles for this habitat would be box, wood, and gopher. The lizards would include fence lizards and skinks, but not the geckos. Most geckos are tropical or semitropical. They would probably freeze before they got the hang of hibernating.

Temperate woodland soil is *not* water-soaked. A container of water is present so the animals can swim and soak, but the soil should not be any more than barely damp.

Temperatures in this realm might naturally include freezing winters, but herptiles can be acclimated to bypass their period of winter hibernation *if* you regulate the length of daylight *every day*. As the period of daylight becomes imperceptibly shorter in the autumn you must shorten the night with artificial lighting and warmth or your animals will shift their internal gears and become lethargic.

Temperate Semiaquatic

This habitat is surely more of a challenge to a pet keeper than a dry terrarium because of the problems associated with nutrient soups. They tend to generate smells and transmit diseases. This is because a nutrient soup is what bacteria love to eat and you can't have one without the other.

So what to do? Arrange the wet part of your setup so that it can be easily drained and replenished

with clean water. Don't plan to "control" bacteria with chemical treatments or antibiotics. That is the wrong way to go. Just reduce the amount of nutrients in the water and let the bacteria take care of the remainder—then you will have the bacteria working for you. Bear in mind that the greatest part of the solid material in your own colon is, in fact, living bacteria. Always was. Always will be. If it were not so, you would be dead or certainly very sick.

Western box turtle, *Terrapene ornata*. This species should be kept in a drier terrarium than other box turtles.

A cluster of green anoles. Never keep two male anoles together, as they are generally aggressive toward one another.

Let's say you want to keep a couple of small semiaquatic turtles in an aquarium. They will want a dry perch. You have several options.

• Place a brick on the bottom of the tank and add water until the top surface of the brick is level with the water surface. Your pets will be able to swim to the brick and climb aboard. Wedge the brick a bit to create a ramp effect. When you want to clean the tank, remove the turtles and the brick and you have only to dump the water and scrub four sides and the bottom. If the brick gets sour, leave it out in the weather for a week or two and it will be as good as new. The drawbacks to this arrangement are that it provides no place for plants and it is not especially attractive from a natural standpoint.

• Fasten a partition across the bottom of the tank to the height that you plan to bring the water. The partition should be a piece of plate glass with ground edges, and it should be sealed in place

16

healthy. Certainly it will not be pleasant.

• Pot the plants and provide a ramp for the animals to crawl out of the water. Be careful that the ramp is placed so that it cannot be dislodged. Many aquarium windows have been cracked when slabs of slate were tipped over. Who did it? The turtle did it or perhaps the butler did it. Does it really matter who did it?

• Remember that many semiaquatic animals thrive by eating each other.

• Remember that some amphibians can crawl straight up the glass sides of an aquarium. They never come back—they always go away.

• Remember that many newts, salamanders, and frogs enjoy cool water. Find out what natural habitat your chosen animal came from.

• Start here with pond turtles like red-ears, maps, spotteds, musks, muds, sliders, cooters. Also keep efts and other newts and salamanders in a semiaquatic habitat.

• The ribbon snake is semiaquatic and so is the common watersnake—usually a mean animal.

• There are not many semiaquatic lizards for your semiaquatic terrarium. To fill the niche, look to the crocodilians—

with silicone cement that you can buy in your pet shop or hardware store. Then you can have plants in sandy soil on one side and water on the other side of the partition. The clean-up would be accomplished with a siphon.

Learn to use a siphon by filling a tube with water; then, with thumbs on both ends, get the discharge end a few inches lower than the suction end. Don't suck a siphon tube; you will surely get a slug of that stuff down your gullet sometime and it might not be

"Many aquarium windows have been cracked when slabs of slate were tipped over. Who did it? The turtle did it or perhaps the butler did it? Does it really matter who did it?"

17

but watch the temperatures.

Tropical Woodland

This habitat is much like the temperate woodland. Here, however, the temperature and humidity will be higher and the amount of light will be of greater intensity and of longer duration. The animals kept here are not accustomed to hibernation, and the plants will grow throughout the year. This is where you will keep anoles and many species of geckos and common green iguanas and orchids.

• A water spray squeeze bottle or pump device is necessary because many of these animals don't drink from ponds or standing water. They drink droplets of dew or rain water off leaves. The standing water can be in a small dish, to be rinsed and refilled whenever it is not clean.

• The range of temperatures here would be from 75°F to 85°F (24°C to 30°C).

Tropical Semiaquatic

This is the most difficult terrarium habitat to maintain because the problems caused by decaying waste are aggravated by the temperature. Bacteria grow faster in warm soup, so you must be certain that your arrangement is easy to flush thoroughly, frequently.

• Crocodilians are to be kept in this environment.

• Softshelled turtles are rarely seen out of water except to lay eggs.

• There are many newts and salamanders that live in water—never leave. Some can be bred easily by hobbyists.

• The African clawed frog is wholly aquatic and does well in home terrariums. Actually the "terra" part for this animal would be only for esthetic reasons. The frog will do nicely in a bare rectangular tank so long as it is well-fed and the water is adequately filtered or circulated or replaced frequently.

• There are some tropical water snakes but I don't recommend them for beginners. Start with something that you can get to like. There are many turtles that will quickly learn to take food from your fingers—I don't suggest that for a beginner with water snakes.

THE NATURAL HISTORY OF HERPTILES

Would you be more comfortable if you had some hard rules about herptiles (reptiles and amphibians)? OK. All turtles have shells, and all species of turtle are egglayers. Those are about the *only* rules that will stick. For example, there are several species of legless lizards and there are several species of snakes with vestigial rear legs (called spurs). There are some lizards with functional eyelids and some without, and one herp (the tuatara) with three eyes (sort of). Reptiles are not slimy, except that if you touch the wet shell of a certain softshelled turtle you will find it to be positively slimy.

Some reptiles can regenerate lost tails and some cannot. Most reptiles have teeth, but turtles do not. Most reptiles get their oxygen just by breathing air, but at least one turtle can extract oxygen from water by drawing it into its cloaca. Some reptiles are vegetarian and some eat only animal products and some eat both.

Some reptiles are silent, but several turtles and at least one crocodilian and at least one lizard (a gecko) are positively noisy. Incidentally, the "voice of the turtle" mentioned in the Bible comes not from a turtle but from a pigeon, the turtledove.

Amphibians and reptiles are called "cold blooded," but this also is not strictly true. Some female pythons incubate their eggs and are able to regulate their temperature somewhat. Some herptiles (snakes and some lizards and some frogs) have forked tongues and some herptiles don't. One has a tongue that will stick out a distance equal

Western box turtle, *Terrapene ornata ornata*. Box turtles are omnivorous, that is they eat both plant (fruit, berries, mushrooms) and animal (worms, snails) matter.

to the length of its body (an African chameleon). Some amphibians have no tongue at all.

Amphibians are all slimy except that some are not. Amphibians lay eggs in water except that some give birth to living young—one frog actually incubates its eggs in its stomach! All herptiles swim or squirm to creep or crawl except that at least one snake and at least one lizard glide through the air and there is one Central American lizard which will literally walk on water.

Some snake venoms are highly toxic, but there is at least one type of snake-eating snake that is itself not venomous and which seems to be immune to the venom of the snakes it dines on.

The variety of herptiles staggers the imagination. For shape, color, habitat, sex life, longevity, diet, and methods of movement, they are unequaled in the vertebrate animal kingdom. You pay your money and you can take your choice.

It is easy to make a rule about animal behavior, but it is difficult to get all the animals to always behave according to the rule. Here for an example is a rule: amphibians want to be near water since their life cycle includes the laying of eggs in wet places. Now, that's a rule. We made that rule only after careful observation and long deliberation.

From that rule we can deduce that a tiger salamander (genus *Ambystoma*) would *always* be found among mosses and ferns and streams and ponds. Right? No, wrong! One was caught as it crept out of the burrow where it had been hibernating—along with some prairie rattlesnakes. The nearby vegetation consisted of drought-resistant pasture sage, cushion cactus, and prickly pear cactus. This account appeared in the pages of *Herpetological Review,* a publication of the Society for the Study of Amphibians and Reptiles (SSAR), and we can be sure it was not part of an elaborate practical joke.

So should you keep your tiger salamander in a terrarium planted with cactus and sagebrush? *No*. And that's a rule.

Food

Terrarium animals should ideally be fed what they naturally eat. Sometimes that is impossible or impractical or too expensive, and then we must look for alternatives or we must reconcile ourselves not to keep those animals. Actually much of this has been worked out by the pet shop industry—animals that cannot be fed in home terrariums

simply don't enter the marketplace. For an example, consider those snakes that eat only lizards or other snakes or eels; this can be expensive, so these snakes rarely show up in pet shops.

The vast majority of terrarium animals will thrive on mealworms, mice, earthworms, crickets, ants, dog food, tubifex worms, whiteworms, and fresh household vegetables such as lettuce, peas, and spinach. Some might favor green frogs or whole small fish or strips cut from larger fish. (You can breed your own crickets, worms, insect larvae, mice, fish, and even frogs, or you can get them by other means. That is a separate subject and will not be treated here. Whole books have been written about how to raise the food that terrarium animals should be fed.)

A few cautions are in order. Not all redworms are earthworms. There is another variety often found in farmyard manure piles which has a disagreeable odor and is often rejected by animals that go ga-ga

Smooth green snake, *Opheodrys vernalis*. The diet of this species consists of insects and spiders.

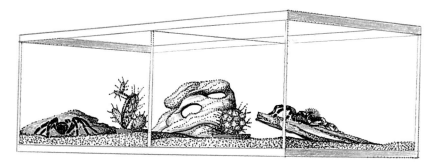

Tarantulas have been known to eat small lizards such as the green anole.

over earthworms. Some people call it a dungworm. Some authors have suggested that it is perhaps poisonous to herptiles.

Canned dog and cat foods are assuredly wholesome; most are packed under supervision of the department of agriculture. If your herptile will eat these products you have a convenient and inexpensive variety to offer. If the can is too large for a single feeding, you can freeze or refrigerate the remainder.

Mice are an important item in the diet of many herptiles, especially snakes in the 2- to 4-foot size range. Many lizards also relish a mouse. For many, it should be dead. It is especially convenient if your snake or lizard will eat a mouse that has been killed, frozen, and then fully thawed to room temperature before it is placed in the terrarium. Very young mice whose eyes have not yet opened are called pinkies; for many herptiles this is what they want—and it is good

for them. Any *whole* organism will contain more nutrients than just muscle or just skin or just liver or whatever.

Snails are often eaten and even relished by turtles. Some salamanders and even frogs and toads will also eat live snails. The red ramshorn (*Helisoma*), apple snails, and garden snails are all good wholesome foods and should be offered. The common garden slugs, which are simply snails without a shell, will be eaten by some herptiles and rejected by many others. There is no harm in trying. Offer slugs to box turtles and American toads. Small ground snakes (*Storeria*) may also take slugs.

Crickets are either black or gray. You can buy black crickets from nine-year-old kids who catch them from under dry rubbish in fields or you can buy both colors by the hundreds from bait dealers who will ship them— yes, by the hundreds— inexpensively and conveniently.

I once fed a colony of African chameleons on gray crickets that were sent to me from, I believe, Memphis, Tennessee. One awkwardness about crickets is that if they escape into your home you may find that they eat your carpets or furniture stuffing. They also tend to be noisy at night.

Newborn mice are recognized as an important food for some reptiles. Again, you can raise your own or find a supplier. Fresh or frozen and fully thawed, they are a clean and nutritious source of protein. Some animal rights activists may threaten you with eternal damnation for feeding mice to snakes. I wonder how they will keep owls and cats and hawks and foxes from eating mice.

Biological supply houses will ship various sizes of live green frogs or you may discover that your pets will accept frozen, freshly thawed frogs—much more convenient that way. There is a problem with the leopard and pickerel frogs. One (the pickerel frog) has a virulent poison in its skin that very few other animals can tolerate. The other frog (the leopard) looks like it.

Toads are all right to keep in some terrarium habitats but they should not be used to feed other animals. Exception: the hognosed snake eats toads and thrives on them; in fact, it eats little else.

Roaches are a nasty word in the kitchen, but many lizards thrive on them. Geckos are especially fond of cockroaches—that may explain why geckos are so popular as "guests" in many tropical homes.

Tadpoles and pollywogs are sometimes relished by aquatic and semiaquatic herptiles. If you have a good supply you might maintain an aquarium of them to assure a supply of live food.

Feel free to experiment. You will discover that, for example, when you breed the axolotl (*Ambystoma*), it will eat a tremendous number of earthworms but that the young will need bits of fresh raw beef liver or they will develop skin hemorrhages, sicken, and die.

Mammal fat is probably the only animal food that these

Turtles vary widely in their dietary requirements—some will eat anything while others will take only molluscs or fish.

creatures will have trouble with. You will find that many amphibians will avidly eat lean red meat and especially liver.

Fruits and vegetables need only be ripe, fresh, and untreated by chemicals. Box turtles enjoy strawberries, melon, lettuce, and mushrooms. A word of caution: the scientific literature tells us that a man was once poisoned by eating a box turtle that in turn had eaten a poisonous mushroom.

Daphnia is an aquatic crustacean, an arthropod, a member of the order Cladocera. There are several species of interest to pet keepers. They look a little like fleas and are often called ditch-fleas or water-fleas. They grow well in alkaline waters that are highly enriched with nutrient substances like horse manure. The name daphnia comes to us from Greek mythology. Daphne was at one time courted by Apollo and, depending on the version you get, she may have been changed into a laurel. What is more to the point is that an unmated female ditch-flea can reproduce itself. Its young might well all be female, and they in turn could produce another generation of females, *et cetera*. The same animal under different conditions could also give birth to male ditch-fleas. There are about 400 species of these little

creatures living in fresh water, and most or all are eaten avidly by small fishes and by many aquatic amphibians. This is an excellent food dried or fresh frozen or, better still, alive. You can keep a culture going for years in an aquarium or a spare bathtub or a garden pond. Live daphnia can be purchased from tropical fish *breeders*. Nowadays few *dealers* bother with this excellent food.

Whiteworms are tiny earthworm-like creatures. They are white rather than pink and they are easy to raise in garden soil mixed with leaf mold and peat. They are fed on stale bread that was soaked in milk. Cooked cereal (wheat or oats) is also a good food for them. Their culture is odorless and costs practically nothing. The worms do best at 60 or 65° F. The soil must be damp but not wet. The scientific name of the most commonly cultivated species is *Enchytraeus albidus*. Small tailed amphibians relish this worm. The largest whiteworm is almost as large as the smallest earthworm.

Tubifex worms are aquatic and were a standard live food for tropical fish in 1930. Today they are hard to come by in many places because few people want to collect and clean them. They congregate in mud near sewer outfalls. Today so much sewage

Smooth green snake, *Opheodrys vernalis*. This is a ground-dwelling species that lives close to water.

is contaminated with dangerous chemicals that it is risky to use this animal as a pet food unless you know that the sewage is safe. In the Orient this is still a standard food for aquarium fishes and is also excellent for small aquatic turtles and amphibians. A good substitute for live tubifex worms is freeze-dried tubifex worms. This product is harvested in places such as Taiwan, cleaned under running water, freeze-dried, cut into convenient little cubes, and sold in pet shops as a tropical fish food.

Artemia are commonly known as brine shrimp. They are little shrimp-like creatures that are accustomed to life in waters saltier than sea water. They come to us as eggs we can hatch and as live shrimp, frozen shrimp, and freeze-dried shrimp. If your aquatic pet will eat them, you are well on your way because they are disease-free and nutritious. They

come to us in several species and in several sizes.

Many herptiles change their eating habits as they grow. For example, larval frogs and toads (pollywogs and tadpoles) will eat algae and similar plant life, but the adult frogs and toads eat only animal life. A bullfrog pollywog will eat vegetable matter, but an adult bullfrog will eat other frogs, small turtles, small birds, mice, moths, flies, earthworms—in short, anything that moves and that it can get inside its mouth.

There are also those that go the other way. Some young semiaquatic turtles will eat only animal matter, but as they mature they will eat large quantities of aquatic vegetation. Even the juvenile common snapping turtle—surely a predator—will be found eating aquatic plants when it weighs 20 pounds or more. Keep an open mind. Be observant. Give your pet an opportunity to teach you something.

I learned about 20 years ago that a captive iguana then living in an apartment in Washington, D.C., preferred Stouffer's brand spinach souffle over all other foods. This quick-frozen product was prepared as if for the table, and as soon as it was cool enough to eat, the 6-foot common green iguana would wolf it down.

Foods for Small Lizards

So many people get into terrarium keeping with an anole or a similar small lizard that a short list of the foods they eat would be useful here.

Mealworms. These are often high on the list of foods that are offered, but sadly they are low on the list of foods that anoles really thrive on. The mealworm larva—the grubby shiny cream and tan creature—goes through several molts before it metamorphoses into the black beetle that mates, lays eggs, and repeats the cycle. Anoles don't eat the beetle but they do eat those larvae. The problem is that after each molting a soft delicious morsel of live food quickly develops a hard covering of shell-like material that an anole finds difficult to digest. If you could pick out the *recently* molted mealworms to feed your pet, the situation would be better. Still better would be a diet with more variety.

Spiders. Anoles and many other small lizards will enjoy eating many varieties of spiders. Of course the tarantula is large enough and powerful enough to turn the tables and eat an anole.

Fruit. Now and then a small lizard like a gecko or an anole will eat a tiny bit of ripe banana if it is offered, moving slowly, on the point of a toothpick. Maybe this is a last resort when no live food is available.

Lizards. Yes, often a lizard will eat another lizard if it is small enough to swallow—even another of the same species.

Crickets. You would have to breed your own in order to get really tiny ones, but that's what this hobby is all about.

Wax moth larvae. There are two species, both of which make good food. These moths invade bee hives. If you cannot buy a starter culture, see your friendly bee keeper. The scientific names of these moths are *Galleria mellonella* and *Achroea grisella* .

Darkling beetle larvae. *Alphitobius diaperinus* is much like a small mealworm and has the same problems.

Isopods. These are multi-legged arthropods also called sowbugs and pillbugs. Pillbugs are apparently distasteful to many or all herptiles. The vaguely similar (but unrelated) centipedes

Wood turtle, *Clemmys insculpta*. This species is mainly carnivorous but will occasionally eat fruits.

and millipedes are eaten by some species, however. It won't hurt to try small specimens of almost any terrestrial invertebrate as potential food sources.

Houseflies. Anoles and many other small lizards will thrive on adult houseflies. Additionally, the maggot that eventually metamorphoses into an adult fly is also a good food for many terrarium animals. British hobbyists have mastered techniques for producing great numbers of these little white grubs. There, pet dealers sell them not only for terrarium herptiles but also to bird keepers. They are called "gentles."

Ants. Choose a variety that doesn't bite. Avoid the large red ants and the fire ants. Horned lizards and their ilk are known to eat only some species of ants.

Fruitflies. Small lizards like geckos and anoles will do well on fruitflies, *Drosophila.* Some

domesticated strains of this insect have withered (vestigial) wings that make them incapable of flight. They creep and hop but they don't fly. This tends to make it easier to restrain them while the lizards are capturing them, but from time to time one or two will escape. If you use the vestigial wing mutation, then you cannot evade responsibility when the little fellows get into the kitchen bananas. Interestingly, fruitflies don't eat fruit. They eat the yeasts that grow on the fruit in an area of broken skin that makes the pulp available.

Water

The plant mister or sprayer is the device that led to success with chameleons. Once they never lived long even when they were feeding avidly. It seems that they only drink by picking up droplets of water on the leaves and twigs. Spray your chameleon once daily.

If your pet shop doesn't sell sprayers, get one from your hardware store or farm supply. Be certain that it is absolutely clean. Insect sprays will kill lizards too.

Snakes and most amphibians—as well as many lizards and turtles—require a shallow bowl of clean water for drinking and soaking purposes. The bowl should be securely

anchored or weighted to prevent overturning and either should be too shallow to allow drowning or have a ramp of some type inside so the herp can readily climb in and out. Except for completely aquatic species (clawed frogs, softshelled turtles), no herptile should be forced to stay in the water all the time. Even watersnakes will come down with fungal blisters if kept too wet.

Dangerous Species

The beaded lizard and the gila monster are the only venomous lizards. Although both are relatively lethargic, a beginner has no business with either of them. Other lizards may bite you. The bigger the lizard, the bigger the bite.

Crocodiles, alligators, and their ilk are often nasty, and they too can inflict a wound on man and beast alike. In one of the nature centers of the Everglades National Forest (or is it a National Park?), there was an alligator that hung out near the boardwalk over the wetlands. He supplemented his diet by eating small dogs, with or without their collars and leashes.

Large softshelled turtles and snapping turtles tend to be mean. They not only bite, they also scratch. Smaller specimens do

make good terrarium pets for aquatic and semiaquatic habitats.

Bufo marinus is a large toad introduced into Florida, Hawaii, and some other areas. Its skin is positively poisonous. The common American toad may or may not cause warts, but surely most predators will not eat a toad—do they know something we don't know?

Some frogs are also poisonous. One example found in the USA is the pickerel frog, *Rana palustris*. Its toxin is so powerful it will even kill other frogs in the same container. The common green frog, bullfrog, wood frog, leopard frogs, and tree frogs are not that

could be killed with the poison extracted from the skin of just one such newt.

You should handle all amphibians with a net or rubber-gloved hand unless you have positive knowledge that the animal is safe. Many also inflict bloody bites on people—a hellbender can really do a job on a person's finger.

After you handle any animal, it is a good precaution to wash your hands, especially if you are prone to sucking your thumb.

Back in the good old days, we had just two kinds of snakes. There were the venomous snakes and there were the non-venomous snakes. The venomous snakes included the cobras and their relatives, the African adders, the rattlesnakes, the coral snakes, the dreaded fer-de-lance, the storied mamba, and the fabled sea snake. On the other hand we had the non-venomous constrictors like the anaconda and the boas of the New World and the pythons of the Old World. Also there were the non-venomous black snakes, indigo snakes, racers, green snakes, corn snakes, bull snakes, milk snakes, and all those other little snakes that one found in the garden. Oh for the good old days when things were black and white and everyone knew which side of the fence one was on.

California newt, *Taricha torosa*. This species has a strong homing instinct in the wild, returning to the same pond to breed time after time.

way at all, but you should bear in mind that frogs are predators and they will eat anything that moves that they think they can swallow. A bullfrog will eat fishes, frogs, salamanders, turtles, snakes, mice, and even birds.

The skin of certain newts and salamanders is highly toxic—perhaps in the same way that certain toads and frogs are. How toxic? Very toxic! In one scholarly report published in *Copeia* [1974, No. 2, pages 506-511] the toxicity of the rough-skinned newt, *Taricha granulosa,* of the Pacific Northwest was described. Between 1200 and 2500 mice

31

A young leopard gecko, *Eublepharis macularis*. Members of this species enjoy an occasional sunbath.

Now consider the following report gleaned from the features section of *Herpetological Review* [Volume 17, Number 1, March 1986, page 6]. Here Andrew Nichols of the Department of Herpetology of the Knoxville (Tennessee) Zoo tells of his experience when a bluestripe garter snake, probably from Pasco County, Florida, bit him on the hand. He did not want to injure the little fellow by forcefully removing it, so he waited three minutes before the snake let go. The finger nearest the bite swelled and turned blue. There followed numbness and other symptoms that are commonly associated with snakebite from venomous snakes.

Remember please that in the good old days all garter snakes were "non-venomous"; it said so in every book. Andrew Nichols goes on in his report to cite some other scientific literature that you may have missed. It goes back to 1978 when Dr. Sherman A. Minton, Jr., wrote an article published in *Natural History* on pages 56–60 of the November issue. Minton described a similar instance where an eastern hognosed snake, traditionally considered to be in the non-venomous category, bit someone and produced a mild version of the typical symptoms associated with the bite of a venomous snake.

Are non-venomous snakes evolving into venomous snakes before our very eyes? No, there is no evidence of that. Are there shades of gray concerning just how venomous is a snake? Yes! First, we know that snake venoms vary in their toxic strength. A drop of copperhead venom might make a person a bit sick, but the same quantity from a cobra could prove fatal. Second, we know that some snakes have sophisticated venom-injection mechanisms with teeth like hinged hypodermic syringe needles and pumps that drive the toxin into the wound. We also know of other snakes not so provided but that get their poison into their victims by chewing rather than puncturing. Third, we know that for these "chewing" snakes the poison is in their saliva.

You are looking at an example of evolution. Each level of sophistication or specialization in this venom strength or injecting business could be thought of as the place where a particular species branched off the Tree of Life over the course of hundreds of thousands or even millions of years.

Charts could be developed that line up all snakes according to their teeth or according to the strength of their venom or according to the quantity of venom, and it will soon become apparent that the old black-or-white distinction is not valid.

Handle every snake as if it were venomous. It doesn't take much more effort and it's a good habit to develop.

Colombian giant toad, *Bufo blombergi*. This species comes from the tropical rain forests of southwestern Colombia.

33

⑤ CLASSIFICATION

To keep track of living things, Carl von Linne, better known to us latinized into Linnaeus, established a system of classification in 1758 that bears his name (the Linnean system of binomial nomenclature). The system has survived these two centuries because it is not frozen by dogma, but rather it permits changes as our knowledge provides new insights. This man was a Swede and a botanist. He wrote in Latin.

In English, the framework of the classification of life comes to us with an easy mnemonic aid. Just hang onto this: *K* ing *P* hilip *C* alled *O* ut *F* or *G* ood *S* oup. The initials of these words give us the general Linnean arrangement.

The first example is the common musk turtle, also known as the stinkpot. The second example is the common spotted

	First Example	Second Example
Kingdom	Animal	Animal
Phylum	Chordata	Chordata
Class	Reptile (reptiles)	Amphibia (amphibians)
Order	Testudinata (turtles)	Caudata (salamanders)
Family	Kinosternidae	Ambystomatidae
Genus	*Sternotherus*	*Ambystoma*
Species	*odoratus*	*maculatum*

Eastern ribbon snake, *Thamnophis sauritus*. Members of this genus are also known as garter snakes.

salamander—the one with large yellow spots on a blue-black background. Let not your heart be troubled with subs and supers or with other arrangements that are not just like this. Just accept the arrangement in principle and let the specialists take care of the details.

The broad brush treatment gives us two classes of terrarium animals, the reptiles and the amphibians. The class of reptiles is subdivided into four living orders: crocodilians, turtles, snakes and lizards, and the New Zealand Rhynchocephalia (for the lizard-like tuatara).

The class of amphibians consists of three living orders. The first of these orders to consider is Caudata—consisting of about eight families of newts and salamanders. All Caudata have tails. The Latin word for tail is cauda. The next order of the class of amphibians is Salientia. Samuel Johnson, in his 1804 Dictionary of the English Language, says "SALIENT...Leaping, bounding, moving by leaps..." Here we find about a dozen families of leaping and bounding frogs and toads. Finally there is that third order, somewhat swept under the pet keeper's carpet. These are the caecilians, the earth dwellers. Most burrow and lay eggs, but at least one gives birth to living young and is aquatic. Caecilians are limbless and, for all practical purposes, blind.

In case you wondered where the word amphibian comes from, consider that from its Greek source we get (amphi = both) two realms—land and water. Most amphibians spend part of their life on land and another part in water.

Not to be confused with the caecilians (which are amphibians), we should be aware of a group of reptilian lizards called amphisbaenids. These animals burrow, have small or no eyes, and have no external ear openings. They grow to a length of a foot to a yard and look like giant earthworms.

You deserve any explanation (and not apology) for why this book is peppered with "usually" and "most" and "about," especially in the natural history and classification sections. You paid a precise sum of hard-earned money for information. You might expect to get a mass of precise information for that money. Well, that's not the way the cookie crumbles. I did try to be accurate, but Mother Nature permitted many genes on many chromosomes to mutate over eons of time. Herptiles, especially, evolved and diverged

"In case you wondered where the word amphibian comes from, consider that from its Greek source we get (amphi = both) two realms—land and water. Most amphibians spend part of their life on land and another part in water."

to best suit living conditions that were not everywhere identical. The various environmental niches were eventually filled with animals that through a process of natural selection became well-suited to their habitats. Often in geological processes over the ages, a mountain or an ocean or a glacier or a deep chasm came to separate two populations of similar animals. Natural selection continued to operate and random mutations continued to take place. Each population—isolated from the other—took its own course of naturally selecting from the various and random mutations that along with recombinations of genes make each of us a little different from another. As we recombine genetic material we tend to resemble one another more, but with every individual reproductive act there is that ever-present opportunity for a random genetic mutation. From that mutation there is the possibility that an individual might be better adapted to its environment than perhaps another individual, however closely related. So the successful one resists more diseases or grows faster or escapes from enemies more frequently or produces more young that survive, mature, and pass on these traits to their young. That's what success in nature is all about.

All right, you ask, what has this to do with "usually," "most," and "about"? Simply this:

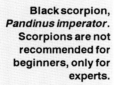

**Black scorpion,
Pandinus imperator.
Scorpions are not
recommended for
beginners, only for
experts.**

because some populations have been isolated for long periods, herptiles tend to be more diversified in form and habit than, for example, birds. All birds have two feet but we know of herptiles with no feet, two front feet, two rear feet, or four feet. So there it is—no feet or two feet in front or two feet in back or four feet. Slimy skins and non-slimy skins and scaly skins, too. Eyes and no eyes. That is one reason why you get a big dose of "usually," "most," and "about."

Another reason for this state of affairs comes from the rules of classification and the people who monitor and apply these rules. They want to be up-to-date with their best thinking about the relationships among animals. Every time a new species is discovered or a new fossil is discovered, there is the possibility that a new relationship will become apparent. This causes constant revision in our arrangement of the twigs and branches on the Tree of Life. Shall there be three branches on this limb or four? Twelve twigs on the branch or 13? I submit that for

most of us "about three or four" and "about a dozen" will be all we really need to know. In another year, or ten, someone will surely demonstrate that the three or four should properly be five and that the dozen is only ten. So again, I say, let not your heart be troubled. Just keep a few herptiles in the largest terrarium you can manage and enjoy them.

A pair of young caimans, *Caiman crocodilus*. This species is a member of the family Alligatoridae; even youngsters are highly aggressive.

Dark toad-headed turtle, *Phrynops geoffroanus geoffroanus*. This species is known as a quiet aquatic carnivore.

37

⑥

REPTILES

Red-eared slider, *Pseudemys scripta elegans.* **This is one of the most popular of all pet turtles.**

This is a class of vertebrate animals. The word reptile is from the Latin and it means "creeping animal." There are in the class superorders and orders and suborders and superfamilies and families and subfamilies, depending on whose classification you read. There are also many extinct forms, including the dinosaurs. If you want to see one version of the whole arrangement laid out, you should get a copy of *Systematic Herpetology: A Synopsis of Families and Higher Categories* by H. G. Dowling and W. E. Duellman.

It is not at all simple. For this book we will ignore certain facts such as the fact that lizards and snakes are both in the same order but that crocodilians are in a separate order. Let's just call a snake a snake and ignore its precise position in the Tree of Life.

For our purposes, reptiles have little control over their body temperature. They are hairless and featherless. Most have scales, all have lungs. They differ from amphibians in that they never need to be in water to breathe. Some are aquatic, this is true—but even the aquatic forms always breathe atmospheric air—so there are no gilled reptiles. Here and now we could easily get snowed under in a mass of technical details that will not help you to maintain a terrarium.

The reptiles we are concerned with are all easy to recognize. Turtles are all toothless and shelled. Some have shells that are quite soft, but no other reptile has a shell and no turtle has any teeth.

Snakes never have four legs, most are completely legless, and none have eyelids.

Lizards usually have legs and most have eyelids. Geckos have no eyelids and legless lizards do exist, but we are fortunate that our language includes "usually."

Crocodiles and alligators are lizard-like but are unusual among reptiles because their hearts are practically four-chambered. Mammals and birds have four-chambered hearts but the hearts of other reptiles are somewhat less complex—let's say that there are not more than three chambers in the hearts of the other reptiles. Also the teeth of crocodilian reptiles fit into sockets located in the opposite jaws. When they grab something, they are able to hold on with great tenacity. Their jaws don't chop food; they just hold on. When a crocodile takes prey too large to swallow, it may

grab a limb and then spin itself rapidly until that limb is torn free from its late owner. Not pretty, but surely effective.

Small specimens do well in large aquariums. They will spend 75% of their time in the water but that water must be kept clean. Large specimens may be domiciled in bath tubs and really big fellows are often given to zoos where the curators are already up to their ears in large crocs. They live a long, long time.

Hatchling South American caimans were once a popular item in pet shops, but today their importation is restricted and the *Salmonella* problem also limits their availability.

So there you have the bare bones outline of the class of Reptiles. Now to look at the orders within the class.

Hog-nosed snake, *Heterodon simus*. When excited, this species flattens its head and hisses loudly in imitation of a cobra.

39

Turtles

There are mammals that look like fishes (porpoises and whales) and there are mollusks that look like worms (shipworms), and there are lizards that look like snakes (glass lizards), and there are crustaceans that look like mollusks (barnacles) and there are even fishes that resemble seaweed (sargassumfish), but there is no turtle that looks like anything but a turtle, and there is no other living creature that even remotely resembles a turtle. The turtle is unique.

More specifically and especially for those of you who read a book from back to front, in the kingdom of animals there is a phylum of creatures with spinal chords called chordates. Most chordates have backbones, so classifiers make these a subphylum called vertebrata. Within this group there is a class of "cold-blooded" scaly animals with lungs called reptiles. Among these reptiles on a small branch of the Tree of Life is the order of the turtles. The turtles are located near the snakes, lizards, crocodiles, and perhaps an additional few borderline groups that survived from ages past as living relics of extinct forms or as intermediates with the amphibians.

Well then, what is a turtle? It is a reptile with a shell to which its ribs are fused. Furthermore, its legs are attached to its backbone *inside* the rib cage. By contrast, look at yourself—your arms and legs are hooked up so that their connections are all outside of your rib cage. To protect my professional reputation, I must mention that there is one exception. There is a sea turtle whose ribs are not fused to its shell. The great class of reptiles is divided into orders and all turtles are in the same order, Testudinata. We thus call all of them testudines (also known as chelonians). There are only about 230 species of turtles worldwide.

How does one get from the order Testudinata to the species in your hand? Well, we have suborders. Cryptodira is the suborder of turtles that pull their heads into their shells by bending the neck *vertically* into an "S" shape. Most turtles do it that way. Cryptodiran turtles are found all over the tropics and in much of the temperate world.

Turtles that bend their necks in a horizontal plane—rather than up and down—are in the suborder Pleurodira. Turtle keepers call them side-necks and these come to us only from the southern continents.

At the next level below suborder we come to families and

then the families are divided into genera (a single generic unit is called a genus). Then in each genus there is at least one species. Species is both singular and plural. The first letter of the species name is not capitalized, and that's a rule!

Looking further at what you have, all turtles are toothless. They have sharp horny sheaths on the jaws, some with saw-like edges, but there are no real teeth. The nearest thing to a tooth on a turtle is a tiny bony pin that is attached to the nose of a hatchling and is used to cut through its leathery egg shell. This little "egg tooth" subsequently breaks off and never reappears. Something like a belly button, it once represented something important, but after birth just a scar remains.

Looking still further, all turtles have leathery skin. None are slimy overall. They do have eyelids. They all have four legs and a tail. They all lay eggs and these eggs are always buried in the ground. The eggs are always whitish and the shells are not brittle but instead are leathery. Turtles have little or no internal control over their body temperature so they must choose their habitat to suit their needs. If it is too hot in the sunlight they will hide in the shade or dig into

the ground for comfort. If it is too dry for too long, some species might also burrow. If it is too cold for their blood to circulate easily or for their food to be digested, many species of turtles hibernate until the weather moderates. Hibernation is a form of deep sleep that takes place underground or underwater, the animal living off its stored fat. If you think in terms of literature, then think of Sleeping Beauty or Rip Van Winkle—almost.

Some turtles will eat any nourishing living or dead substance, animal or vegetable or fungus. Some other species are fussy eaters, but most of those available from the pet shops or caught in North American ponds and woods will chop up and eat avidly just about anything they can digest. There is even a recorded instance of a man who was poisoned by eating a turtle which had recently consumed a poisonous mushroom.

From another point of view,

Red-eared sliders, *Pseudemys scripta elegans*. Male sliders are smaller than females but have elongated claws on their forelegs.

41

perhaps worlds away from your own, consider the turtle as did the philosophers of the Orient in days of yore. They told us that the earth was supported on the back of a turtle and that this turtle simply stood, sustained in the universe by its dignity. Some American Indian legends are similar, but in them we find the warning that when and if the great turtle should tire of this, he might just sink into the vast universal abyss of mud from which he rose with the world on his back and take this whole shebang with him. So watch out!

In the meantime we have the pleasure of their company in most of the tropical and temperate lands of the world and many of the seas as well.

The list of turtles suitable for captivity as pets grows ever shorter when we delete those that are protected by law. Some species are very scarce and would quickly be wiped out if every collector could bring a few home. Let's face it—after all is said and done about our good intentions, most animals that we tamper with end up rare or endangered or extinct, and those we leave alone generally manage to survive and reproduce and hold their own.

When you find a turtle in the woods or in a pond, don't tell yourself or anyone else that you will take it home in order to do it a favor. That simply won't wash. A native turtle doesn't need your hospitality. Perhaps it does need your protection from other people, but generally speaking a box turtle (for instance) will live 60 or 80 years with no direct human help or hindrance. Furthermore, if it is left to its own devices, it probably will be a parent at least a few times during its long life.

There still are many species of small, hardy, common, inexpensive, attractive, amusing, quiet, and odorless turtles available from or through pet dealers. These animals make fine cage pets, aquarium pets, house pets, garden pets, and ornamental pond pets. Some are natives of the tropics and need a hothouse environment to thrive, but others will do nicely even in New England or southern Canada—caged inside in the winter and in the garden during the summer. There are some that do best in a cactus desert and others that favor a swamp or a bog or a prairie or a woodland glen. If you read this before you get a turtle, so much the better. If the turtle came before the book, you should at least be able to take better care of what you have. Fortunately, many people have admired and studied turtles before this book came along, so there is an abundance of additional literature if you want to learn still more about the natural history and care of these reptiles.

The most well known terrestrial turtles native to the U.S.A. are the gopher tortoises and the box turtles. In Europe a Greek tortoise is popular as a pet.

The lower shell, known as the plastron, of a box turtle is hinged; it can be closed, thus the turtle gets its name. A few other varieties of turtle also have hinged shells; in fact there is one whose top shell, known as the carapace, is hinged.

The largest of the terrestrial turtles are found on remote islands in the Pacific and Indian Oceans. Some are really tremendous and can easily carry a child for a ride on their backs. Most are rare or endangered and virtually all are protected.

The wood turtle of North America looks like a terrestrial turtle but it actually favors a habitat where it can dabble in a bit of water from time to time. This is a handsome species, and many pet keepers consider wood turtles to be especially intelligent. It is protected in many areas.

There are several native U.S. turtles that are protected and may not be captured or handled in commerce. Since there are so

Red-eared slider, *Pseudemys scripta elegans*. Sliders are found in large lakes and rivers as well as in small ponds and brooks.

43

many that are not protected, there is little reason to go after the rare ones.

Are some turtles ever bred in captivity? Yes. There have been turtle farms producing turtlets for the pet trade and eggs for fish bait in the lower Mississippi Valley for many years. Can you breed and raise your own colony of turtles? Yes. Don't start today and expect instant success; a turtle might need to be three or more years old and female and fertilized before she might lay a few eggs that might take six months to hatch. If you want to make money and you have a little to invest and you have a choice between a turtle farm and a savings account, I recommend the savings account.

Probably the best known terrarium herptile from 1920 to 1960 was the red-eared slider turtle, *Pseudemys scripta elegans.* It was surely the first pet of many millions of young people in the U.S.A. It was also the pivot point of a great deal of controversy and of governmental regulation in the pet industry. Actually, for the pet keeper, all species of this genus and similar genera can be lumped. Together one or another type of slider, map, or painted turtle can be found in every area of the U.S. east of the Great Plains. These turtles were

sold in pet shops and in the pet departments of the five-and-dime stores all over the country. A turtle was a dime and a turtle bowl was an additional 15 cents in 1928.

These turtles were sold as hatchlings sometimes hardly out of the egg. Some would still have the belly scar where the yolk sac was connected. Many were coated with a paint much like fingernail polish and embellished with fanciful designs. These cost an additional 15 or 20 cents. Of course the little painted animals were destined to die, and if they survived for any length of time they would be deformed because the paint acted as an external skeleton and prevented normal growth of the shell. This was a stupid and cruel thing to do to any animal.

To make matters worse, the turtles to satisfy the market were deliberately crowded in turtle farm ponds. There they were fed on waste scraps from slaughter

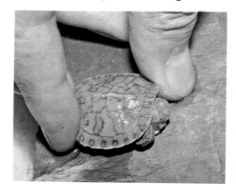

A newborn red-eared slider, *Pseudemys scripta elegans*.

44

houses and fish processing plants. A bacterium (*Salmonella*) present everywhere was highly concentrated in these ponds. Large doses of *Salmonella* cause gastric disturbances in people. They become nauseous, feverish, and sometimes even dehydrated because of diarrhea. Some species of *Salmonella* bacteria in the right concentrations can even cause death, especially in children.

Well, over the course of years the painting of turtles was stopped largely through the efforts of the animal welfare and humane societies, but the *Salmonella* problem was not addressed for another 20 or 30 years. Really, it wasn't a genuine problem at the turtle farm level because this bacterium is found everywhere anyhow. Anyone who had a "clean" turtle in a dirty turtle bowl could breed his own *Salmonella*. Nevertheless, the government stepped in, partly because of an attempt by one turtle farmer to corner the market by promising a "clean" product that, when the chips were down, he couldn't deliver.

The outcome of all this was that today the little aquatic turtle is no more an article of commerce. If you want one, you will have to catch your own or trade with another turtle keeper who caught

or bred a few.

Although the *Salmonella* story is historically tied to cooters and sliders and sawbacks and red-ears and map turtles, the regulations today also apply to all aquatic and semiaquatic species. Land tortoises are still legal in pet shops because they are not kept swimming in *Salmonella*-laden waters.

What we are supposed to be protected from is the possibility of disease transmitted from the turtle water to a person. For example, a little boy sticks his hand in the aquarium and then sucks his thumb or kisses the turtle or takes it with him into his bathtub. One might wonder how

Painted turtle, *Chrysemys picta bellii*.

45

they cannot catch enough animal life to sustain themselves and partly because a larger animal doesn't need as much concentrated protein to sustain itself.

All these turtles except, perhaps, the softshells will want to come out of the water from time to time to bask in direct sunlight or its equivalent. This exposure helps them get rid of leeches and algae and other parasites. Also, the sunlight provides the ultraviolet (UV) radiation necessary to generate vitamin D. Without this vitamin, no amount of calcium will suffice for bone growth. Be aware that ordinary window glass, plate glass, polished plate glass, and aquarium glass stops virtually all the UV present in sunlight. Deprived of UV, these animals will still do very nicely *if* their diet includes food that contains vitamin D. There is a lot of this vitamin in the liver of an uncooked fish. That is why in this book and most other instructions to pet keepers you will notice that the author says *whole fish* first and then mentions strips of fish meat. Don't filet a fish in order to feed a terrarium animal unless that fish is too large to feed as a whole. If you must cut up a fish,

much help we should get from do-gooders and from our government to protect our health. Remember that these disease-causing bacteria are everywhere all the time. They become concentrated and thus dangerous in *any* warm liquid containing nutrients. A housefly lands on the rim of a bowl of chicken salad and in a few hours the *very same bacteria* will be multiplying in a geometric progression. Should we ban the eating of chicken salad at summer picnics?

Keep the water clean in any terrarium, aquatic, semiaquatic, or terrestrial, and wash your hands before you suck your thumb. To say more would be like beating a dead horse.

These turtles, and also mud and musk and the painted and the spotted and the snappers and the softshells all eat earthworms, small fish, and pieces of fish. Also, large specimens of some species will supplement their diet with plants, probably because

you should try to include some of the liver in what you offer to your captive pets.

Crocodilians

Crocodilians are lizard-like and all have four legs. An overall view of a crocodilian, that is a crocodile, alligator, caiman or gavial, is that it is tropical or semitropical. It is semiaquatic, and many species are normally found in brackish water or pure sea water. It is carnivorous—it eats no plant matter. It lays eggs. It has relatively large scales, and its tail is relatively stout. The hind feet are webbed to help it swim. The ear is covered with a flap like the tympanum of a male frog. Many, perhaps all, species have a voice that develops in the adult to a substantial bellow. The largest might reach nearly 30 feet in length. There are 21 species living on earth today. In ancient times there were surely many more— the fossil record makes this clear. The pupil of the eye is elliptical (like a football) and is arranged vertically (like a football standing on end).

Crocodilians are ranked at the top of the evolutionary ladder among reptiles because their hearts have four chambers.

For many years the native American alligator was protected because it was endangered. During that period many South American caimans were imported to satisfy the pet trade. Today the alligator is no longer considered to be endangered in all parts of its range. The caiman is, like the aquatic turtle, considered to be a transmitter of *Salmonella,* so it is no longer readily available in pet shops.

Crocodilians, if you can obtain one nowadays, should be kept in a terrarium that permits the animal to get completely out of the water whenever it wishes. The water must be changed frequently. You cannot rely on bacteria to consume uneaten food and fecal matter. Temperatures should range around 75°F (24°C). Although these animals need warmth to assure prompt digestion of what they eat, shade should also be available.

A crocodilian 1 foot long should be in an aquarium *not less*

One of the many "true toads," *Bufo canorus*. Members of this genus can be found in most areas of the world.

than 2.5 feet long and 1 foot wide. If you care for it properly, it will grow rapidly. If you cannot accommodate a large crocodilian, you should not possess a small one. Zoos end up with a surplus because pet keepers bit off more than they could chew, and "crocs" tend to live a long time.

Feed a young caiman or gator on whole fish, frogs, strips of lean beef, and large earthworms (night crawlers). They also will eat mice, rats, and road-killed animals.

You would be well advised to freeze any road-killed animal and then let it thaw to room temperature before feeding it to your pet reptile. This will reduce the hazard of introducing parasites.

Lizards

These are the reptiles with eyelids and without shells but not including the crocodilians. The lizards are dry-skinned, scaly, and most (but not all) have legs. Some have forked tongues, some have blunt tongues, and some have sticky tongues that they can extend for the length of their bodies in order to capture an insect or even a small bird. Some lizard scales look like tiny beads and not at all like scales. Two species of American lizards are venomous; the others are not, but a large lizard can inflict a dangerous bite or lacerate a person with its spiny tail. Their size ranges from tiny geckos that can perch on your finger to monitor lizards that weigh several hundred pounds. Some are carnivores, some are herbivores, and some will eat whatever is offered.

The most popular pet lizards for beginners are anoles, tokay geckos, iguanas, skinks, curly-tails, and spiny lizards.

Snakes

There are a few legless lizards, true. There are a few snakes that have small leg-like spurs at the base of the tail. There are a few caecilians that might be confused with snakes if you ever encounter one, but that's highly unlikely. Everyone knows what a snake is—simple: it looks like a snake. Oh yes, an eel is a fish, not a reptile. It is slimy and it has no lungs. Some eels are found crawling through grass on damp nights, but, nevertheless, an eel is still a fish. Then there are the sea snakes. Most of them are totally aquatic and cannot survive out of water, but they are truly reptilian snakes, even though their tails are flattened rather than circular in cross-section. But really that doesn't matter because you cannot keep them as terrarium,

pets. For one thing, they are very, very poisonous. Now—leaving out sea snakes and other poisonous snakes and those that are rare and/or endangered, what have we?

We have about 340 species and subspecies of snakes native to North America. Of them, perhaps 50 are commonly kept as terrarium pets. Some of the 340 are very rare and protected. Others are venomous and thus dangerous. Still others are burrowers in the earth and so offer nothing for us to view. Others are too nervous to restrain in a cage.

Still others have very specialized dietary requirements—one, for instance, eats eels. But for all those that are not good pets, there are plenty of others that are easy to tame, interesting, and long-lived. Some are even bred in captivity by hobbyists. Start your snake-keeping by talking to your pet shop proprietor.

Remember that snakes naturally eat living food. If the thought of this repels you, keep a terrestrial turtle or a common green iguana and avoid this aspect of the natural process of life.

Juvenile Chinese water dragon, *Physignathus cocincinus*. This species is also called the green water dragon.

49

Amphi means both. It is derived from the Greek, and it tells us that these vertebrate animals go through a life cycle that includes time in water with gills and in air with lungs. Of course there are all sorts of exceptions.

Well, what can we hang our hat on to describe an amphibian to a Martian? Start with the hope that there are amphibians on Mars and you are off the hook.

Some give birth to living young and some lay eggs. Some seem to skip the water phase of their lives. Some are slimy and some (such as toads) are dry and rough-skinned. Some seem to have minute scales embedded in the skin. Some have tails and some do not. Some adults are small enough to perch on your

thumb and others grow to a length of several feet—the giant salamanders of the Orient grow to nearly 5 feet long and close to 100 pounds in weight. The African goliath frog will grow to a length of a foot, *not* including its legs. There is tremendous variability. Most have four legs but some have two and some are legless.

Frogs

When you have kept frogs for a while and you begin to think you know something about them, I suggest you assume a position of humility because the last word on frogs has yet to be written. For example, there are frogs that carry their eggs around in a spongy tissue on the back of the *male* until they hatch. All right, you accept that. Now how about a male frog that incubates his young in his vocal sac? Now there is even some well-educated speculation that he not only incubates his young but may even nourish them.

You may have decided that you are interested in frogs but not in toads. I suggest that before you firm up that decision you

Western toad, *Bufo boreas*. Members of this species can tolerate saltwater habitats in the wild.

read the following section of this book.

Toads

Toads are like frogs, only different. They are alike in that they are both in the same order—Salientia (now more often called Anura). Toads and frogs are the leaping amphibians. Everyone knows how they differ. Adult frogs tend to be slippery and adult toads tend to be dry-skinned and warty. Surely you know that.

The typical frog lays a cluster or lump of jellied eggs in water and the typical toad lays strings of jellied eggs in water. Kids call a larval frog a pollywog and a larval toad a tadpole, but most of us would be hard put to tell one from the other.

One way to separate toads from frogs is with a snake that eats frogs. Excepting the hognosed snake, which eats toads almost exclusively, many snakes that eat frogs will not eat toads. Toads excrete a poison from their skin glands that in certain instances has been known to have killed foolish dogs. Annoyingly, there is a famous frog from South America known as the poison arrow frog because the Indians use its skin to prepare arrow heads which assure the quick death of any bird or mammal they

hit. Then of course there is the poisonous pickerel frog of the U.S.A., so on consideration we cannot separate frogs from toads by way of poison.

Let's take another look at this question of frogs and toads. Which is which? Worldwide, there are about 2700 species of leaping amphibians. Some are found north of the Arctic Circle! They are highly variable in life style and in appearance. There are smooth-skinned toads and as mentioned before, poisonous frogs. Some of those 2700 species even lay their eggs on land. I suggest we think of frogs and toads together and not separately.

Eurasian common toad, *Bufo bufo*, taking shelter under a mushroom. Healthy toads are known to have large appetites.

Newts and Salamanders

Let's lump them since, like

51

frogs and toads, the distinctions tend to be blurred except to the specialists. These amphibians have tails throughout their lives—frogs and toads usually lose their tails as they metamorphose from tadpole to adult.

Newts and salamanders are in the order called Caudata. Cauda refers to the presence of a tail. Most have four legs, some lack hind limbs. Juvenile forms often have conspicuous gills that disappear at metamorphosis and are replaced by lungs. Some Caudata go through life with gills, and still others can switch. The male does not inject his sexual products into the female;

that is to say, there is no copulation, but in some species fertilization is internal. Pretty tricky? Yes. Of course, there are some exceptional cases—most lay eggs in water but several give birth to living young. Several place their eggs in earth rather than water.

None eat vegetable matter. Most enjoy whiteworms, tubifex worms, earthworms, and small insects such as fruitflies. Aquatic forms will eat mosquito larvae, daphnia, and brine shrimp. None want to be in brackish or salty water. Some like really cool water—say 55°F. None bask in hot sunlight. Some have poisonous skin.

⑧ HOUSING

Note the tidy arrangement of this terrarium. Never make the bathing area too deep, for tank inhabitants have been known to drown.

If there were no aquariums, terrarium keepers would have to invent them. A conventional glass aquarium—four sides and a bottom, water tight, easy to clean, relatively inexpensive, and attractive in many settings—is the ideal container for small herptiles, mammals, and arthropods. In case you have forgotten, an arthropod is a creature with paired, jointed limbs and an external skeleton. Crabs, spiders, and insects are all arthropods, by far the largest phylum in the animal kingdom.

If you come onto an aquarium that is reported to "leak a little," it may still be perfectly adequate for a desert or dry woodland habitat. Your friendly pet shop dealer might even sell you a tank with a cracked bottom for your dry-land animals. Of course you can make repairs with silicone cement, but if the glass is actually cracked, it should not be subjected to any water pressure. All you must add is a glass or screen cover and a secure closure.

Can you build your own

terrarium? Yes. Should you build your own terrarium? No. Start with something simple, tried, and true. Don't invent the wheel. Ten years down the line, when you are more experienced, you might be ready to build your own. Don't jump the gun. There is plenty for you to do *inside* the terrarium.

Outdoor Enclosures

The one exceptional arrangement that sometimes works even for a beginner with herptiles is a garden enclosure for turtles. The rules are simple to spell out but may not be so simple to apply.

• The enclosure must be underground as well as above ground. You must ditch at least 18 inches and install a corrosion resistant screening like chicken wire or galvanized hardware cloth to keep your pets in *and also* keep their enemies out. This is more easily said than done.

• The animals you choose should be native to areas with a similar climate or you will need to provide inside housing for the "off" season.

• The enclosure must be closed on top unless all you want to keep are turtles and terrestrial toads.

• If the enclosure is not closed on top, it must be higher than three times the greatest dimension of the largest captive turtle. Yes, a 4-inch turtle will climb a wire mesh cage, at least a foot, before he falls or tires. If there are other animals outside or small children nearby, then the cage design should be based on how high *they* can climb. Think also about dogs, cats, rats, mice, opossums, raccoons, and skunks.

Terrarium Plants

Plants for a terrarium need to be rooted. Like the animals, they too have temperature and light and moisture requirements. You must decide if you want an animal or two in an arboretum or you want a few plants in your terrarium. Either way is OK. That choice is yours *but* the choice of *which* plants is limited by the environment you choose. No need to belabor the point. You might well begin with your local pet shop. Describe the habitat and then review the

A true chameleon, genus *Chamaeleo*. Members of this genus should be kept in tall terrariums, as they need to climb.

An albino American toad, *Bufo americanus*. The habitat of this species should contain some hiding places.

selection. Bear in mind that terrestrial turtles and some iguanas are omnivores or herbivores. (That means that they eat all sorts of things or that they eat herbs, that is vegetation, plant life, fruits, vegetables, plant stems, leaves, and even the pulp of a cactus.)

Here are a few suggestions— use your imagination:

• Anoles and geckos go well with orchids.

• Newts and salamanders make one think of moss and ground pine.

• Woodland snakes may be kept in cages or tanks with Spanish moss, sphagnum moss, peat moss, or even grass sod dug out of a garden.

• Small desert lizards make one think of cactus, century plants, and aloe.

• Woodland lizards seem to go with rough tree bark, twigs, and flat stones.

• Crocodilians go with flat stones. Bear in mind that absorbent wood and brick cannot be thoroughly cleaned.

Heat and Light

A 25-watt incandescent light bulb produces about as much heat as a 20-watt electric heater. If you

55

really want just the light, go to fluorescent tubes. If you want to supplement the light with warmth, perhaps the light bulb would be a perfect source for both.

The use of a light bulb is good for several reasons. Days are usually warmer than nights anyway, so this use will mimic nature. You can adjust the size of the bulb and also the distance from the bulb to the animals. You can place the bulb where it will illuminate and heat only part of the terrarium. In this way you will quickly find out what level of light and heat your pets prefer. You can replace the bulb easily and inexpensively when it burns out.

Yes, you can immerse a light bulb in water—not the base, just the glass part—but the risk of a short circuit is ever-present and really the hazard of electrocution is ever-present. I must acknowledge that I have in the past heated terrariums and aquariums with immersed light bulbs, but this only proves that I have led a charmed life—and even I don't do it anymore.

Humidity is associated with cage covers and heat sources. If your slimy-skinned amphibians need more moisture in the air, you would logically go to a glass cover, but a desert habitat for a spiny lizard would surely get a screened cover.

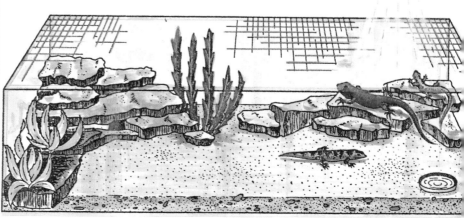

Try to arrange your terrarium so that it contains several different temperatures. That way, if one side is too cold, the inhabitant can move to a warmer spot.

56

9

HERPTILE HEALTH

Many authors of books like this will offer a chapter titled "Diseases," and I've done just that many times in these past 35 years of writing about caged animals. Perhaps, however, it's a mistake to think in terms of waiting for disease in order to control or cure it. It will be a great deal easier on your pet, and on you, to anticipate problems and do something to *prevent* disease.

Since this book is a primer for the keeping of many creatures, the suggestions must be of a general nature.

A few words about salt and salinity might be appropriate here. Salt is a compound, sodium chloride. As we know, it is soluble in water; the oceans of the world contain salt in a concentration of about 3.5% by weight. This number is often presented as 35 ppt or 35 parts per thousand—obviously the same as 3.5 parts per hundred or 3.5%. How should you make terrarium water salty? Well, you could carry home sea water if you lived nearby and had easy transport, but it really is not necessary. Your pet shop probably handles sea salt. This is derived from evaporation of sea water and it contains *all* the trace elements present in the ocean—sodium chloride just being the major constituent.

How much to use? Well, a *fluid* ounce of water weighs about one ounce. That's how a pint manages to weigh a pound, the world around. Thus, a gallon weighs 128 ounces. A tablespoonful of salt weighs about 0.6 ounces, so we get a fraction of 0.6 times $\frac{1}{128}$ or about 0.48%—a bit less than .5% of salinity in that gallon of water. That, as you can see, works

Green anole, *Anolis carolinensis,* chomping on a cricket. Proper diet will go a long way toward keeping your herps healthy.

Keep in mind that the proper humidity level will make it much easier for your pet to shed its skin properly.

minute bath.

Vinegar in terrarium water is useful in the prevention of fungal diseases. It seems that many of these infections never get started if the water is very slightly acid, and vinegar seems to be a natural way to achieve this acidity. If you add one part of ordinary white or yellow kitchen vinegar (not with wine or spices) to 20 parts of terrarium water in an aquatic or semiaquatic habitat you might never have any fungal infections on your pet. Vinegar in stronger concentrations is used to *cure* many fungal diseases—it has been used as a bath, for two or three days, in a proportion of one part vinegar to one part water. That is really strong medicine. It may work when other treatments fail, but you should never start out with a treatment. You should, instead, start with simple, intelligent hygiene. Don't crowd your pets. Remove all wastes and uneaten foods promptly. Remember that a dozen pond turtles might well occupy a natural body of water ¼ acre in extent. Even one in a 30-inch by 12-inch aquarium concentrates a lot more turtle in the water than nature intended. An acre, you may remember, is about 43,000 square feet; that aquarium would have an area of 2.5 square feet.

So, there are two inexpensive

out to about 15% of the concentration of salt in the average ocean water sample, and that's just on the light side of perfect for a diamondback terrapin. Remember, this is *not* 15% salt content, this is just 15% of the amount of saltiness of sea water. Bear in mind that average sea water is only 3.5% salt—and approximately 76.5% water by weight. If you double the dose to two tablespoons per gallon there will be no harm; it might even prove better for your pet.

Should you use a salt bath for amphibians? No. Amphibians have porous skins and the salty water could cause fluid imbalance and lead to death. Should you wash a turtle in brackish water from time to time? Yes, if only to assure that any leeches would be thus eliminated. Should the water in every turtle terrarium always be brackish? No. A brackish water environment is recommended for just the diamondback terrapins. The other species would get an occasional 30-

substances to help maintain animal health. But what if you acquire a badly infected animal— can it be saved? How? Consider a trip to your veterinarian. This will cost real money, but you will get professional help for the specific problem. It is not easy to diagnose many of the diseases that your pets might have.

One popular antibiotic for a wide range of diseases is aureomycin. You might introduce it with food or in the bath water. A veterinarian might elect to inject this or a related remedy into your pet.

Some flies—the bot is a good example—will place their eggs in a reptile's skin and the maggot or maggots will form a lump. You or the doctor might be able to lance open such a lump and remove the maggots. The resulting wound would be treated with an antiseptic and then left to heal.

Eye ailments often result from malnutrition—obviously they will recur until the diet improves. One effective cure is a cream or salve containing terramycin.

A 5% tincture of iodine is often recommended for fungus except around the eyes. I suggest that a treatment with vinegar should be attempted first. If it doesn't work, then try the iodine.

Soft bones, deformed shells, and the like are almost always a result of calcium and vitamin D shortages. Be sure your pet gets to eat *whole organisms* and supplement its diet with exposure to direct unfiltered sunlight or short duration exposure to ultraviolet light or small quantities of vitamin D in some food supplement.

Mouth rot in reptiles is a relatively rare disease and it is treated with a sulfa drug that you may find through your pet dealer or veterinarian. It is sulfamethazine in a 2.5% water solution. Mouth rot generally develops after an injury as a small white spot inside the mouth. Untreated, it can destroy bone. It is contagious.

Ticks and mites are bothersome parasites. You can get rid of them by one of two methods. Suffocate them with a coating of oil—like petroleum jelly or olive oil. If that doesn't work, try a remedy you can purchase called Dri-Die. It absorbs moisture and it will dry these pests to death. People who work with cage birds sometimes use Dri-Die. Of course you should avoid any product containing DDT. If used incorrectly, Dri-Die can kill a small reptile, so follow manufacturer's instructions and be careful.

Sometimes a snake or a lizard cannot molt when it should. A

"Soft bones, deformed shells, and the like are almost always a result of calcium and vitamin D shortages. Be sure your pet gets to eat whole organisms and supplement its diet with exposure to direct unfiltered sunlight . . ."

59

snake's eyes will get cloudy and its whole mood will become mean. Place the animal in a slightly damp linen or burlap bag for a week and the skin will likely be shed with no additional problem.

A beginner should avoid making any attempts to physically peel skin from a reptile about to molt. Just give it a place to absorb moisture and perhaps a surface to rub up against, then let nature take its course.

Skin blisters of fungal origin may form on aquatic reptiles— check the water. If it is not slightly acid, make it acid with a little vinegar. Use litmus paper to find out. Litmus turns pink in acid water and blue in alkaline water.

If a herptile has an incurable disease, one humane way to put it out of its misery is to place it in a bag and place the bag in your home freezer. Just remember to remove it before some hungry person gets inquisitive.

Temperature and humidity will have a lot to do with herptile health. Each of the creatures on earth fills a niche that no other creature fills quite as well, so if you offer something in your terrarium that is absolutely perfect for one species of snake, it probably will be less than absolutely perfect for all other snakes. This is a slight

exaggeration because some creatures cohabit similar niches but have different diet requirements or different spatial needs. An American toad would be terrestrial and a tree frog would look for twigs, branches, leaves, and bark—but both could do well in the same temperature and humidity. Also the toad would eat more "earthy" foods such as slugs, earthworms, and beetles, while the tree frog might go through life never having tasted an earthworm but having consumed more moths than that toad ever saw. Give this fact of life some thought if you want to keep more than one animal in each terrarium. If you don't, there will be conflict or one animal will be afraid to eat or one animal will eat the other—and being eaten is surely an aspect of animal health. Remember that a medium size bullfrog can easily swallow a fully grown mouse or two or perhaps even three.

Another thought about temperature for you to consider is that in nature, and that's what this is all about, there are few places where daytime and nighttime temperatures are the same. Evenings tend to be cooler. If your terrarium is heated by electricity and the control is a simple thermostat rather than a clock thermostat, then the effect will be

Red toad, *Bufo carens*. Members of this genus are susceptible to several parasites. Therefore, hygienic cage maintenance is a must.

a relatively uniform temperature for all 24 hours. You might well discover that your pets do better if the nighttime temperature is cooler by say 10°F than the daytime temperature. If your pets are vigorous and have a good appetite, you are doing it right. If they are inactive, limp, and eat poorly, you might well check that temperature.

As a herptile molts, it may eat its shed skin—snakes do not, but some lizards and most amphibians might. Don't concern yourself so long as the molt is complete. If a few patches of dead skin remain and a few days have elapsed, give your pet a dip in some clean water or spray it with some room-temperature water. You don't want to scald or freeze your little animal; just get the skin to slough off. Turtles and frogs tend to molt in patches under normal circumstances, so bits of adherent old skin are not unusual.

A healthy herptile will molt periodically, one layer of skin each time. Now and then you might encounter a snake that accumulated two outer wrappers before molting successfully. Often the problem was one of poor nutrition or inadequate occasional moisture.

Tails are sometimes a problem for herptiles. Of course adult frogs and toads are tailless, but for the rest there is no firm rule. Some lizards (and some salamanders, too) will let go their tails when they are fighting or when they are being chased. Mother Nature arranged it that way, it seems, to permit the animal or at least the most important part of it to escape. The tail that dropped off will twitch violently and is supposed to divert the predator from the main course while consuming the appetizer.

What are you to do? There is nothing you can do. The tail will not re-attach. Perhaps it will grow back. Perhaps it will partially grow back or perhaps it will not grow back at all. It depends on the species, its general health, its age, and so on. Turtles do not lose their tails this way—neither do crocodiles. If you lift a turtle or a crocodile by the tail you may well cause a fatal injury. Geckos and glass lizards are famous tail droppers. Rattlesnakes rattle their tails but don't drop them.

If a pet lizard drops its tail you should simply watch and assure yourself that no infection invades the injury and let normal healing or regeneration proceed.

Semitropical lizards and tree frogs will probably do well at 75 or even 80° F, but most northern forms of tailed amphibians, frogs, and toads do best at temperatures near 70° F, minus 10° or plus 5°. The diseases of amphibians seem to go along with elevated temperatures, crowding, unclean water, and alkaline waters. Peat moss or a little vinegar or tea might suffice to keep the water on the acid side—get some litmus paper from your friendly high school chemistry teacher or buy a test kit from your pet dealer and check the water from time to time. It is good insurance.

Red-leg is a serious frog disease. It rarely strikes a large, clean, cool terrarium with very few specimens, especially if the water is slightly acid.

Profile of a green anole, *Anolis carolinensis*. Before purchasing your pet, check for missing scales, skin, and limbs. Never buy a deformed animal.

OBTAINING SPECIMENS

Start your thinking by thinking small and safe. For starters, you have no business with any crocodile or lizard more than 3 feet long and no constricting snake over about 6 feet long. If you have a large constrictor, there should be a full length mirror in the room where you keep the animal—you may need to unwind the snake someday and you may not be able to find an end, especially if something is getting snug around your throat.

Avoid all species that are nippy, poisonous, or prone to drop their tails.

What remains? Dozens of species of native herptiles and several dozen more of exotic varieties available through your pet dealer or through advertising in the publications of the various herpetological societies. Join one, go to meetings, and *listen* before you give a long speech about your box turtle that eats strawberries from your fingers—every terrarium keeper can top that. Through the societies you will find specimens to trade or purchase.

Check before you go out and catch one of the endangered and rare whatchamacallits that will cost you a whopping fine and a black mark on your police computer file card. The vast majority of small herptiles are not protected. Find out if there are any that are dangerous. Go out on your first trip with someone who is experienced.

A pair of long-tailed salamanders, *Eurycea longicauda guttolineata*.

INDEX

Inside front cover: Giant Tree frog, *Litoria infrafrenata.* Photo by Jeff Wines. **Inside back cover:** Baby slider turtles, *Pseudemys scripta dorbignyi.* Photo by H. Schultz.